# Father Richard M. McAlear, O.M.I.

Fr. McAlear is a native of Boston, Massachusetts. He entered the religious order of the Oblates of Mary Immaculate in 1960, studied in Rome and was ordained there in 1970 after receiving degrees in Philosophy and Theology. He returned to the United States, taught high school and received his degree in Religious Education.

Fr. McAlear became involved in the Catholic Charismatic Renewal in 1972 and entered into full-time healing ministry in 1976. This work has taken him to every part of the United States, as well as Asia, Central and South America, Canada, Ireland, and Australia.

Fr. McAlear's gifts of teaching and healing are powerful indications of the healing love of Jesus Christ being poured out on today's world. He is much in demand as a speaker for retreats, conferences, and seminars. He is also a popular pilgrimage director who has led hundreds of pilgrims to the Holy Land, Marian Shrines, and on many other journeys.

Since 1977, Fr. McAlear has been a member of the Association of Christian Therapists. He is a past director of Our Lady of Hope Center in Newburgh, New York, where healing prayer and charismatic ministry were combined with a strong outreach to the poor and needy of the area.

After 10 years in Washington, DC as Vocation Director, he has recently been released to devote himself to full-time preaching and to the healing ministry.

He can be reached via e-mail: FRMAC2693@aol.com. Fr. McAlear's schedule, along with other information about his ministry, can be found on his web site www.FrMac.org.

# *Forgiveness*

## Experiencing God's Mercy

### NEW AND EXPANDED EDITION

*Richard M. McAlear, O.M.I.*

# Forward

This small work on forgiveness has been in process for several years now. It has been rewritten, enlarged and revised several times. This present edition is the fruit of much thought and prayer. Since I teach and preach widely, as well as speak at retreats and conferences throughout the country, there has been a fair amount of feedback to my teachings, usually in the form of questions. This always occasions more reflection and insight into the vital issue of forgiveness. It seems that there is nothing more important and nothing more defining than the teaching on sin, forgiveness, pardon and guilt.

The original insight, that occasioned the first edition, was that forgiveness is necessary for healing and for spiritual growth. Nothing cripples spiritual and emotional life more than unforgiveness. To be unforgiving is to be paralyzed emotionally and psychologically, as well as spiritually. Nothing impedes the work of God in a soul more than resentment. Forgiveness is spiritual health.

Further reflection reveals that forgiveness is the very heart and soul of the Gospel message itself. Forgiveness defines Jesus in both His teaching and His work. He cannot be understood without coming to grips with this central aspect of His ministry, which is most also His identity. Jesus is forgiveness and forgiveness is Jesus. His name is mercy.

Finally, in this present moment in history, the unique message of Jesus stands out more clearly than ever. There is another spirit abroad in our day that presents quite a different image of God and a totally different theology of sin and redemption. Two contrasting visions in stark relief present us with an essential choice. Is God a God of vengeance and retribution, a God of punishment and chastisement? Or is He a God of forgiveness and mercy, a God of compassion and pardon? This is the essential question that defines not just one's image of God, but the believer's attitude and behavior in the following of God. Some would see destruction and death to the non-believer as honoring God. Jesus would see compassion, love, mercy and forgiveness – to believer and unbeliever alike - to be the greatest honor given to God. Each approach, in its own way, is seen as an imitation of God's own attitude and behavior.

The Christian, now more than ever, needs to give valid proof and witness to a God of love and mercy, a God who forgives. If that is the God we believe in and follow, then that is the kind of believer we would want to be. People of mercy who forgive as Jesus did and as the Father does are the practicing Christians who make a difference.

This small work attests to the importance of forgiveness in religion and in life.

I want to thank all those who helped make this work possible. A special thanks is owed to Jim Amrein and to Annette Marvin who were the soul of patience and generosity in helping to give birth to the book. To the Oblates of Mary Immaculate, my own community, for their support through the years. And finally, to Cammy Keissler who makes sure that records are kept and that the book is distributed.

ISBN: 978-0-615-22331-5

# Contents

# Chapter 1

## *The Necessity to Forgive*

Forgiveness is the living heart of the Gospel. Reading the Scriptures, we learn that forgiveness includes all that we mean by grace, love, mercy, redemption, and salvation itself. In fact, if we do not have an understanding or concept of forgiveness, we have not yet grasped the core message of the Gospel. It is that simple.

The Gospel story that best expresses this key to Jesus' message is the parable of the man who has his debt requited. It is about a man who owed a tremendous amount of money but was unable to pay back the debt. The master had mercy and out of sheer compassion canceled the entire debt. That same man, now relieved of his financial burden, met a fellow servant who owed him a small amount of money. Rather than show mercy, he had his fellow servant, along with his wife and children, sold into slavery in order to pay the debt. When the master learned of this, he was greatly angered. He said to the ungrateful servant, "I have forgiven your whole debt. Could you not have shown mercy and forgiven another?" (Matt. 18:21-35).

Within that question resides both the gift and the challenge of the Gospel of Jesus Christ. The gift is mercy. The challenge is to be merciful.

First of all, we learn that forgiveness is a gift that we receive freely from God in Jesus Christ. This is the foundation on which all is built. Then, secondly, forgiveness is a command that we receive from Christ. This is the natural result of receiving forgiveness – the need to forgive others. It is out of the experience of being forgiven that we reach out with forgiveness to others.

Other than love, one of the most commonly used words in the New Testament is forgiveness. It is a consistent and basic theme throughout the teachings of Jesus. In the Gospels, Jesus usually links prayer with forgiveness. For example, in the Our Father we pray: "Forgive us our sins, just as we forgive those who sin against us" (Matt. 6:12). In another place, Jesus said: "Whenever you stand praying, forgive if you have anything against anyone" (Mark 11:25) and "Go first and be reconciled, then offer your gift on the altar" (Matt. 5:24). Then there is the severe warning, "If you do not forgive others, the Father will not be able to forgive you" (Matt. 6:15).

Jesus proclaims the grace of forgiveness, then gives the command to forgive, and finally warns about unforgiveness in the heart.

If we block the flow of forgiveness by refusing to forgive, we frustrate the movement of the Spirit. "What you receive as gift, give as gift" (Matt. 10:8). Forgiveness is the first and most important gift that we receive from the Cross of Jesus. He came for mercy. If the flow of forgiveness is blocked, the flow of the spiritual life is blocked, as is the flow of healing. The gift of mercy must be reflected outward if there is to be an authentic spiritual life. Forgiveness received is to become forgiveness shared. Here is a key to the Gospel, as well as to healing and holiness. Yet, it is often an overlooked and underappreciated aspect of the message of Jesus.

There are good religious people who believe, practice their faith and are very devout, but who then miss the message of mercy. Too many acts of violence are carried out in the name of God. Many of the most serious conflicts in the world take place in Christian countries between Christian people. It is all too easy to see violence as a Muslim problem. It is much more widespread and includes Christians, as well as others. Bosnia, Serbia, Rwanda and Ireland are all current examples. It is as though the core of the Gospel message never penetrated the human heart, or perhaps was never truly preached. Certainly, it never made a real difference in personal behavior or in daily life.

In these ongoing violent conflicts, the issue is always forgiveness and the lack of it. Atrocities are usually in retaliation for a previous atrocity, which were in response to some other atrocity. The cycle is self-perpetuating and so continues for years and generations. Vendetta is hatred kept alive. This is true not only in Ireland, Serbia and Bosnia, but also in places such as Rwanda, Kosovo, the Middle East, Sri Lanka and Cyprus, to name just a few. Iraq and Israel are places where the ongoing violence has come to define the culture.

The United States experienced the horrors of September 11 because some people harbored hatred and nurtured the desire for revenge in their hearts. Their anger and rage festered and grew until it gave birth to an act of violence beyond our imagination. Can we imagine a response to this tragedy that seeks justice without mindless revenge? Can the Gospel of Jesus show us a different way to respond that brings peace and not more hatred and violence?

When there is violent conflict in the world, the United Nations can send in peacekeepers to keep people apart; they can build walls to separate them and impose sanctions to intimidate them. None of these solutions address either the actual problem or the cause of the problem. They are all external attempts at solving problems that are internal. We are dealing with matters of the heart. Hatred, revenge, resentment, and retaliation are nurtured in the human spirit and kept alive for generations. Forgiveness alone can bring healing, reconciliation, and peace. The Gospel is all about these qualities that elevate the human spirit.

The anti-Gospel of our day is terrorism that preaches violence as a form of honor to God and as a remedy for perceived hurts and injustices. Rather than being a solution, terrorism plays on the basic instincts of the human heart and breeds nothing more than further pain, injustice, tears and heartbreak. The cycle of death, destruction and chaos becomes a self-perpetuating reality. Sometimes the cycle spirals out of control and becomes outright war and physical violence. Most often the cycle is more subtle, but just as deadly in a spiritual way. Broken and strained relationships, wounded hearts, retaliation, passive aggression, bitterness and inner rage are all products of an unforgiving heart.

Whether it is a nation or a family or a community, it is the same destructive dynamic at work. Unforgiveness in the heart produces nothing positive and everything negative. Too many friendships are destroyed, families split apart and relationships ruined because of unforgiveness. The fruit of unforgiveness is always bitter and has no redeeming value. Everyone loses. Division and heartache are the only lasting results of an unforgiving heart.

## Conflict Resolution—Jesus' Style

The only way to break this vicious cycle and bring healing and peace is with forgiveness. Jesus preached forgiveness as a sign of the presence of the Kingdom of God. He was defined in His day by His compassion and forgiveness. He showed in His preaching and in His actions that it is mercy that is important and essential to the Kingdom of God.

What issue so infuriated the Jewish leaders that they decided Jesus had to die? Why did they want to destroy Him? It was not because He cleansed the leper or healed the sick. It was not because He multiplied bread and fed the crowds. The key issue was that Jesus forgave sin. Remember that the charge against Him before the Sanhedrin was blasphemy. "How can this man claim to forgive sin? This is blasphemy!" (Matt. 9:2-3; 26:65-66). For the Jewish people, forgiveness came from God and always came with a price —chastisement and the punishment due to sin. Jesus, however, forgives freely and generously. He exacts no revenge. He does not condemn. He does not punish, nor chastise. He acquits the guilty. This was important enough to anger and infuriate the religious leaders of His day.

Think of the story of Zacchaeus in Jericho. He is the one who climbed into a tree to see Jesus. As a chief tax collector and public sinner, the people hated him. But when Jesus passed by, he showed Zacchaeus mercy, love, grace, and forgiveness. He accepted Zacchaeus without condemnation. For this the people were angry and murmured against Jesus. Meanwhile Zacchaeus faded into the background while Jesus bore the brunt of their anger (Luke 19:1-10). Jesus welcomes sinners and shows them compassion. It is for this He will suffer.

In another story, Jesus was accepting and kind to a sinful woman. The self-righteous were angered and wondered, "How could He let this woman touch Him? Doesn't He know she is a sinner?" (Luke 7:36-50). There was more than surprise and dismay; there was an angry response because mercy and forgiveness were given so freely. From Jesus there was no punishment, no condemnation. He shows only mercy and kindness. But grace and love are seen to be stumbling blocks, not causes for rejoicing. The perversion of the human heart prefers punishment to forgiveness. The heart of Jesus shows only mercy.

**The Sticking Point**

What was true in Jesus' day is still true today. For many, consciously or unconsciously, the lavish mercy of God is a sticking point in the whole Gospel message. Everyone desires mercy and pardon for themselves, but has a difficult time seeing others receive forgiveness. Of course this is the central message, not just a marginal part of the Gospel. Forgiveness is not some optional devotion; it is the Good News itself. Jesus *is* the Mercy of God.

In Jerusalem some years ago, I was doing a seminar in Biblical studies. During that time in the Holy Land, I had occasion to discuss Jesus and Christianity with followers of Islam (Muslims). Mohammed and his followers have a deep respect for Jesus. They regard Him as a great prophet and accept many truths about Him. They believe, for example, in the Annunciation by Gabriel to Mary and the Virgin Birth of Jesus. They believe in His miracles and even the Ascension. What they do not accept is the forgiveness of sin. They can accept that Jesus was crucified, but not that it was for the remission and pardon of sin. They would always come back to the same point, "Someone has to pay. If you sin, you must face the consequences". Forgiveness, freely given, is not just. Justice demands retribution and punishment. For them, a God who forgives so freely is just weak and feeble.

This helps explain Middle East politics today. There can be no mercy or forgiveness. The rule is "an eye for an eye, a tooth for a tooth". Justice can be harsh. Forgiveness is seen as weakness. The fact is it takes much more inner strength, maturity and depth of spirit to forgive than to punish. That insight is not as evident as one might think. People demand that sin find atonement, punishment and retribution. Forgiveness and pardon seem to be too easy and too simple a solution, lacking in justice. Is there a cost to forgiveness?

Of course the Christian answer is that someone did pay and did satisfy the demands of justice. It was not the sinful, however; it was the innocent who paid. Jesus, as Redeemer, took upon Himself the sin of the world and suffered the Crucifixion. He set us free from the demands of the law and reconciled all humanity to the Father. Because of His Cross and the shedding of His Blood, sin is forgiven. There are no preconditions. It is a gift. It is grace, truly amazing grace. Jesus, by the Cross and the shedding of His Blood, meets the demands of justice on behalf of us all.

Many who are paralyzed by unforgiveness do not adequately understand the grace of forgiveness. It is a gift, received only to be given and shared. Something deep in the darkened soul still resists forgiveness and demands justice and revenge, chastisement and punishment. That is true also with one's self. Guilt, with its self-hatred and unworthiness, is all too common. At its core it is simply a denial of forgiveness and mercy.

To go into an intensely emotional situation such as Northern Ireland, Israel and the West Bank or Iraq and preach forgiveness could be foolhardy and dangerous. How would such a message be received? Would the messenger survive? Two famous people were killed in the Middle East—Anwar Sadat and Yitzhak Rabin. Both were killed for the same thing. Each had chosen the path of peace, reconciliation, and forgiveness. Neither was killed by the enemy, but rather each by his own people. The path to peace, which lies down the road of reconciliation and forgiveness, was abhorrent to some people. War, violence, and retaliation were preferred. Two men died violently because they believed in forgiveness and acted on it. We desire peace and reconciliation and reject the only way to bring it about. This is a strange contradiction in the human spirit.

The vendetta dies hard. To speak of mercy and forgiveness in clear and practical ways can be dangerous. It can lead to the Cross—suffering, rejection, and even death.

Is it possible to speak of mercy and forgiveness to Holocaust survivors, to the victims of racism, to the oppressed, or to those who suffer unjustly from rash judgment, gossip and rejection? Could those wounded and traumatized by the events of September 11 hear a message of mercy and forgiveness? Would such a message be received? Could it be heard?

Yet, as difficult as it may be, there is still something in the human heart that yearns for forgiveness. We instinctively know that sin needs to be touched by mercy. There is no other solution.

The Good News of the Gospel is the proclamation that God has forgiven us, freely and without reservation. In return, we need to forgive. It is all free gift, unmerited and undeserved. It is sheer grace and is called mercy. Mercy is deeper and richer than forgiveness. It touches on the transcendent mystery of pure love.

If someone apologizes and says, "I am sorry", the response is to forgive. Jesus mentions this in the Gospel, and the issue immediately becomes the limits of forgiveness—how much and how many times must one forgive? The answer is as plain as it is difficult: forgiveness is to be without limit: "If your brother or sister should harm you seven times, and if seven times they come back and say, 'Forgive me', then you must forgive" (Luke 17:4). In fact, it should reach seventy times seven times, or in other words, infinity. There are no limits here.

Forgiveness is in response to an apology, and there is no measure to it. It must be abundant and from the heart. Forgiveness is a great gift, but there is more. Mercy goes even further than forgiveness because it is unsolicited and undeserved. It is pure grace and gift. Some things are actually unforgivable, but are embraced by mercy. Sometimes, mercy is required because the people to be forgiven never asked for it, would not appreciate it, and actually do not deserve it. When injury is deep and painful, the injured one could claim justice and withhold forgiveness. Some things do seem unforgivable. Some actually are. Terrorism, with its senseless violence and its endless toll of innocent victims, would seem to fall into this category.

However, this is not about rights or justice in human terms. It is about mercy. We are confronting here the essence of the Cross, which is at the very heart of Christianity. Jesus died for the forgiveness of sin. The Cross is the instrument of mercy. St. Paul calls the Cross both a stumbling block and an obstacle. To show mercy demands a stretching of the heart and an enlargement of love. Mercy is the language that love speaks. It is the victory of God's love over justice and condemnation. Mercy triumphs over justice, we learn in the Bible. This is understood by the mature of spirit, and we all strive for it, but try as we might, not all attain it. We usually want mercy for ourselves, but justice for others. But forgiveness is necessary for growth and healing. When we consider the impact of hurt, injury and sin on our lives, we need the healing found in forgiveness. We begin with forgiveness and grow into mercy. Mercy must be brought to bear if there is to be spiritual maturity that supersedes justice. This is the heart, the core and the essence of all Christian spirituality.

**I Am Forgiven**

The Gospel does not begin with the command to love and to forgive. Although forgiveness is spoken of often, there is a prior truth. It is the truth that I am forgiven. This is the joy of the Good News—God has forgiven me in Christ. This is the truth that needs to be embraced in the depths of the soul. "For those who are in Christ Jesus, there is no condemnation" (Rom. 8:1). Whatever mistakes I have made, God holds nothing against me. He does not remember the past; He only proclaims forgiveness in the Cross of Jesus Christ, His Son.

When the gift of mercy is received, it makes it possible to forgive another. There is a flow: receiving forgiveness and showing forgiveness. When someone never experiences forgiveness, the result is to project the perceived condemnation of an unforgiving God onto other people as one's own unforgiveness and judgment. There is no flow of forgiveness, mercy, and love. Judgment replaces love and the image of God is distorted. God is forgiving and loving and Jesus is His gift of mercy.

The key to the transforming power of the Gospel is that God has shown mercy through Jesus Christ. Once forgiven, I can forgive. What is received as gift is given as gift.

**Forgiveness and Healing**

Forgiveness is very much a part of healing. There is evidence that we cannot experience healing unless we forgive. This is evident to me from long experience.

Christ instructs us when we stand before God in prayer to forgive our brother/sister from our heart, letting go of any injury. If we do not forgive, we cannot be forgiven; we block the movement of grace. Unforgiveness has two significant effects. One is that it blocks the flow of healing. If there is resentment, bitterness, and unresolved anger in my spirit, it clogs the spiritual arteries and healing love cannot flow. It is like a spiritual stroke and it is deadly. If there is any unforgiveness in the heart or spirit, then healing cannot penetrate. We must choose to forgive deeply if we are to experience the healing love of God. Love and anger cannot occupy the same heart space at the same time. It is like darkness and light, one contradicts the other. The greatest blockage to healing is unforgiveness. Forgiveness opens the door to healing.

When I first started praying with people, a woman with cancer came for healing. After talking with her, it became evident that she was bitter. She was estranged from her sister. There had been a falling out between them over their inheritance. She came to a Healing Mass twice a week. At one point in the course of ministry, I said to her, "You seem angry at your sister". She replied, "Yes, I hate her and I want to see her burn in hell". I told her, "You cannot be healed of this cancer unless you forgive your sister". She thought about that a moment and said, "I'd rather have cancer".

She had a choice. She did not have to feel any great love toward her sister, but she had to let go of the resentment. She eventually did, but it took her months. That was my first insight into the fact that some people carry hurts that are so deep that forgiveness might have to wait. In these cases, to say, "Certainly I forgive you", can be cheap and ineffective when it is shallow and glib. It has to be worked through and owned. Forgiveness must be as deep as the hurt. The woman was eventually healed of her cancer, once she worked through her resentment and chose to forgive. It was a process that required prayer and patience.

The second effect of unforgiveness, at least in some cases, is that it can be a cause of sickness. Resentment is a poison in the soul that ultimately infects one's whole being. These are the sicknesses that begin in the spirit, influence the mind and emotions, and ultimately manifest in the body. Bitterness, unforgiveness, unresolved anger and resentment are all poisons. They eat away at our spiritual and mental health, often developing into physical illness as well. We must be aware of the impact of unforgiveness on our bodies as we seek healing.

The spiritual and physical aspects of our being are deeply interconnected and affect each other. Psychosomatic illness is real sickness. If illness has a psychological or spiritual origin, it does not mean that it is not a true sickness. It does mean that there is a deeper source of the illness that needs to be touched first if there is to be healing. Anger is one of these deep sources of illness that needs to be addressed. Not just in prayer ministry, but in the medical profession itself, there is a deepening awareness of the interaction between the spirit and a person's physical well being. Anger is found to be an important contributor to ill health, both physical and mental.

Thus, healing and forgiveness are deeply linked to one another, first because unforgiveness blocks healing as it impedes the flow of the love of God, and secondly because it can be the origin of disease.

**Forgiveness Is a Decision**
Forgiveness is a decision that we make. It is a choice of the will. It is not a feeling. We do not need to feel forgiving or loving. We cannot expect that the next time we see the person we forgave that we will like them and want to give them a hug. If we are waiting to forgive until we feel loving, we might wait a long time. Rather, we choose to let go and we decide to forgive. It is a one-way process, a matter of the will. It is not an emotion and it is not necessarily reciprocal.

Sometimes reconciliation is not possible. Perhaps the other is closed and not responsive. Whatever the situation, forgiveness is still called for and is necessary. Only forgiveness will free the heart from the poison of resentments that threaten health, both spiritual and physical.

Reconciliation requires a mutuality that forgiveness does not. Forgiveness has to do with a choice of how to manage anger and hurt. It is a personal decision. In the confessional, when a person talks about resenting someone, often the priest might say, "For your penance, pray for that person". That is both sound spirituality and good psychology. How does one know when there is forgiveness? It is when one can wish the other well and bless one's enemy, then the heart has forgiven and the spirit is set free.

Let me put it in stark terms. Imagine being at the Last Judgment and someone who caused you terrible injury in your life or hurt you deeply stands before God for judgment. There will be a decision about sending this person to eternal punishment or ushering him/her into eternal life. Suppose God were to ask you, "How do you vote?". You might want to see this person burn in hell for what he/she has done, but forgiveness moves you to say, "Let it go. I hold nothing against him/her". You may still want to be in a part of heaven separate from them, but you do not ask for revenge or retribution. You do not even ask for justice. You wish him/her well; you ask only the blessing of mercy. With such a decision, you set yourself and the other person free. You know that you have forgiven.

Jesus told us that we have a choice and whatever we bind on earth will be bound in heaven and what we loose will be set free (Matt. 18:18). Choosing unforgiveness can bind people and hinder their spiritual journey. By choosing forgiveness they are free to move towards life, conversion, and possible reconciliation. Those who are not forgiven cannot grow until they are released. If they are not forgiven until they show repentance and ask forgiveness, then there is a trap without escape. Mercy breaks open the trap; mercy sets everyone free.

The Gospel tells us that our choices have spiritual impact on others. By extending forgiveness, we can set someone free to grow, to love, to move in truth and seek forgiveness. Conversely, we can bind people by refusing to forgive. In such a case, we always bind two people— the one we will not forgive and oneself for being unforgiving. One thing about unforgiveness is that there is no positive outcome anywhere—the other person is not blessed, the situation is not resolved, and we are not free as long as we carry the grudge deep inside.

Sometimes Christians will say, "Well, I forgive you. Let's let it go". This can be a surface forgiveness for appearance's sake. If it is shallow, it is not owned and does not go as deep as the hurt. If the hurt is deep, forgiveness has to go just as deep. It must reach to the depth within where the pain is felt. We cannot carry a deep hurt in our heart and simply offer a shallow forgiveness that is glib and empty. That is not forgiveness, but denial. To say that the hurt does not matter, when it does, is not truth. To forgive from the heart is liberating. There is acknowledgement of the hurt, release and freedom.

## The Deepest and the Worst Hurt

When we own the pain and hold it in our hands, we can begin to own the forgiveness in a deep place. That is most difficult when the hurt revolves around betrayal, the deepest and most painful hurt. This is because we can only be betrayed by someone we love. Betrayal is a broken trust. If we have loved someone and trusted deeply, and then the trust was broken and used against us, that is betrayal. The effects are devastating, because people who have trusted and been hurt are very slow to ever trust again. Yet, if we are going to move into forgiveness, we need to trust. It is a moment of grace when we can rise above the pain and anger and are able to offer mercy and forgiveness. When we speak of forgiveness, we are involved in a profound process that must touch all of the effects of betrayal and untangle them. It is not easy, but it is always worthwhile.

Forgiveness is the gift of freedom that we hold in our hands. We can choose to give it or withhold it. We remember that what we bind on earth will be bound in heaven. It does not just mean up there in the sky, but into eternity, bound until we set it free. God has set us free; He binds no one. Because we are not bound by God, we are free to make decisions. We cannot blame others or say, "Well, I wasn't free". We are free to make choices. We can decide: "I don't want to hold onto this; I want to choose to let it go. I want to begin the process of untangling the emotional pain". At the beginning, that is good enough. Choosing forgiveness is the beginning of the journey to wholeness and life. Feelings will follow, but the process begins with a decision to choose.

Another important element of the unwillingness to forgive is our deep desire to have someone recognize our pain and understand our suffering. That is why some people keep talking about their hurt; they want someone to know how badly they feel and how unjustly they were treated. They cannot let it go, but they must let it go. That is the choice that is needed to make the journey to wholeness. Once that decision is made, the road to healing is open. The journey can begin. Once we have acknowledged the necessity to forgive, and decide to forgive, we then proceed to forgiveness of self, of the other, and of God. This process will be considered next.

# Chapter 2

## *The Way to Forgive*

There are three dimensions to forgiveness because there are three persons that must be forgiven: God, myself, and the ones who have caused hurt.

**Forgiving God**

The first one that needs to be forgiven is God Himself. The spiritual life of too many people is blocked from healing and growth because they find it hard to trust or to forgive God. If we find it difficult to trust God completely, we must consider whether we need to forgive Him. To attain meaningful growth, it is necessary to struggle with God over a variety of issues. One may refuse to face them so as to avoid a confrontation with God or rather than admit to any resentment towards Him. To be angry with God seems to go against piety and devotion. If someone chooses to ignore these issues, however, deep conflicts will remain. They have to come to light and be addressed if there is to be growth. When hurts are not resolved, but simply buried alive, they come back to haunt us in some way.

There are two universal cries of the human heart that God hears every day:

- We demand of God: "Where are You? Where were You when I needed You?"
- The other is the same thing in a different way: "Why did you allow this to happen?"

When Jesus on the Cross cried out to the Father "Why have You abandoned me", He echoed the heart cry of myriad people through the ages: "Where were you? Why didn't you answer my prayer?". A little boy prayed for his puppy and the dog died. A girl prayed for her sick friend and there seemed to be no answer. Someone prayed for a need and received no obvious response. People go through hell in a relationship and ask: "God, why did you allow this? Where were you? Why didn't you stop it? When I was growing up in this horrible situation, where were you? When all this abuse was going on, where were You?".

These cries of the heart, and many like them, are all deeply felt and belong to the human condition. These cries are real; they affect us every time we pray. We may say: "God, you did not hear my prayer. We prayed for so-and-so and they died anyway". Or, "We prayed about this and you didn't seem to respond or intervene". Then the next time we pray, these experiences will influence the quality of the prayer. We will not be able to pray with as much faith or fervor. We will harbor some doubt, buried in a little corner of the mind that says: "Well, He is probably not going to listen anyway". There is a loss of expectancy in prayer, a lessening of hope, and a weakening of trust in God's providence and love. Experiencing the silence and seeming absence of God has practical consequences in one's prayer life.

A serious problem is created when we demand that God constantly prove His love. We can personally witness a miracle, yet two days later say: "What have You done lately?". That is very human. It is nothing more than basic insecurity. We need to be reassured constantly of His presence because anxiety is so deeply embedded in the human heart. Constant reassurance is demanded.

We encounter, in this way, the Mystery of God, spelled with a capital "M". We cannot explain God, where He was, or why He did not intervene. We do not know why prayer was not answered as expected. The frustration for the human mind is that we cannot understand the Mystery of God, who is infinite. Anyone who believes in God on any level of faith must accept one thing: God is Mystery. God is beyond any human power to comprehend, understand, manipulate or control. We all would like to control God, but His ways are not our ways. He does not allow Himself to be reduced to human terms. A God we can understand is just too small. God's love is so great and immense that it can encompass the mystery of the Cross and still be love.

It is said in the Psalms: "The Lord is my buckler and my shield" (Ps. 91:4). It does not say: "God is my butler" as in, "God, please do this. Thank you. Now do that. Thank you. The following is a list of things I would like you to do tomorrow". That is not the way it works; that is not the way of faith. Rather, in my humanity and my smallness, I come up against the Mystery of God and I bow and say: "Your will be done". He is beyond my understanding, beyond my comprehension. He is immense and eternal, beyond my likes and dislikes and greater than what I can see or not see. I must let God have His Mystery. When I die, I will see it all, and it may take an eternity to understand why some things happened and others did not. Right now I cannot reduce God to human size, nor can I enlarge my mind enough to fully comprehend Him. That is why there is faith. It is the only way to heal the fears and anxieties of the human heart. Faith gives peace. Surrender with trust brings healing.

I knew a Pentecostal minister who had a ministry of intercession. He was a holy man who seemed to truly hear God as he prayed for certain things, such as a person's healing. Once as he was praying for someone all night, he heard God say to him: "You make the decision whether this man should live or die". At that moment he had insight into the life and death of the man—what would happen if he lived or if he died. The options were so complicated that he was paralyzed. He could not choose because of all the repercussions and implications that life or death would bring to the person, to other people, and to family and relationships down through the generations. When he began to perceive all that, he was overwhelmed and said: "God, I cannot choose. You must decide". We see things simply and in one dimension. We pray for one thing only, expecting one response and seeking one result. However, with the mind of God, we would see infinite results, repercussions, and implications that are completely beyond all human comprehension. That is why we surrender to Him in faith, trusting in His love.

When things do not work out according to our own desires or needs, we may feel that God let us down or did not answer. It might seem that He was not there and did not show love. All these things we can hold against God when we say: "Where were You?". We need to forgive God in these circumstances. This forgiveness, then, is an act of faith surrender. It imitates the agonized prayer of Jesus in the Garden: "Not as I will, but as You will it" (Matt. 26:39). Our forgiveness is a humble acceptance of God's greater wisdom and love.

**Forgiving Others**

Forgiving others is the part we all think about when forgiveness is mentioned. We all know about being hurt and needing to forgive. It is a universal human experience. The difficult truth is that forgiveness is necessary because there is something to forgive. Because there is hurt, there is need to forgive the injury that caused the hurt. Although this may sound strange, we must forgive injuries, whether real or imagined.

There are real events, and then there is what we feel happened. If we believe it happened, then we deal with it and must let it go, whether it is real or not. The event may be experienced in a distorted or exaggerated way. But if something caused hurt, it is real enough because it had an effect. Forgiving is for all things that were done or not done, actions and omissions, injuries and indifferences.

What was done - such as betrayal or rejection - caused deep hurts, which requires deep forgiveness. What was not done - as in abandonment by people who were not there, words not spoken, support not given, care not shown—this also needs to be forgiven.

In the Garden of Gethsemane, Jesus faced both kinds of hurt. One was active: the real betrayal of Judas, a man whom He trusted and whom He chose as one of the Twelve. Judas sold out his friend and, with cruelty, betrayed Jesus with a kiss. The other hurt (which may have in fact been worse for Jesus) was what was not done and did not happen: "Stay awake and pray with me. I need you". They fell asleep on Him; later they ran away and left Him alone. Among those who abandoned Jesus were Peter, James and John, the three men who were the closest to Him during his life. They, too, fell asleep; they were not there for Him. At the moment of His arrest, they fled like all the others. Yet, more than anyone else, they are the ones who should have been there.

If we need someone to be there in a moment of need, we look to the people to whom we are close, to those we call our friends. We can only be hurt, truly and deeply, by people we love and who love us. If a stranger says something slanderous about me, I would probably feel: "Who are you? I do not care what you think". It may bother me, but not as much as if a fellow priest, a classmate, or friend said something slanderous about me. One I can shrug off because I do not know the person; there is no connection or relationship. The other is a close friend, someone whom I trust. That is the deep wound. It says in Scripture: "If an enemy had done this, I could take it, but it is you, my friend, with whom I shared my bread" (Ps. 55:13-15). Real injury comes from people who should know better, people that know us well. If they betray us, it is a deep hurt and terribly painful. Healing can take more time because trust must be rebuilt.

Think of a marriage that ends in divorce. The most painful part is that on the altar, the two actually gave their hearts to one another. Then one person takes the other's heart and breaks it. That is a painful wound that heals slowly. It would not hurt as much if one's heart were not entrusted to the other. This is the vulnerability of love. One might say: "I am not going to give you my heart because you might hurt it", and thus try to form a relationship without giving the other anything meaningful, so as to be protected from hurt. Then there really is no love relationship. If there is to be love, there has to be vulnerability; it is in the nature of love. We can only be hurt by people we truly love. Much of forgiveness has to do with forgiving people seven times a day, even seventy times seven times a day. These are people who live in community, in marriage or in a family, sharing life. Forgiveness is required; it is necessary; and it is demanded of us. Jesus said: "You must forgive your brother or sister from your heart ..." and do so many, many times over (Matt. 18:35).

Forgiveness starts with letting go of that which I hold against the other. Love does not keep accounts. Paul tells us: "Love is patient, love is kind ..." (1 Cor. 13:4-7). The first quality he mentions is patience. It is interesting that patience should be first. There is nothing romantic there, just the realistic understanding that people have been hurt, they can hurt others, and they must be forgiven patiently in love.

Love keeps no record of wrongdoing, no list of injury, because forgiveness from the heart means always starting over without the burden of past injuries remembered and stored up. Forgiveness, when real, is a freedom for the heart and allows relationships to grow. It is love made manifest.

**Forgiving the Worst Enemy**

Finally, we have to forgive our worst enemy: our own self. That is the hardest one to truly forgive. Toxic guilt is terribly destructive. Lack of self-esteem, guilt and a sense of worthlessness are epidemic in our world. One reason is that we each know how sinful we really are. That is the mystery of the brokenness of the human spirit, deeply rooted in every human heart. When looking at self, one sees mainly faults and failings rather than goodness and beauty. Looking at faults, failings, mistakes and sin blocks the vision of the goodness, beauty, holiness and truth that is also in each human heart. To get beyond self-accusation, we need self-forgiveness. If God has forgiven us, what right do we have not to forgive ourselves? If God accepts us just the way we are, what right do we have not to accept ourselves just as God does?

Some years ago I read the book, *The Diary of a Country Priest.* It was very popular during the time I was in the seminary. It is the journal of a priest, chronicling his spiritual journey with all his conflicts and struggles, along with the lessons he learned over the years. In the last entry of the book, he records that he had finally come to understand that the greatest pride is to hate oneself and the greatest humility is to love oneself. His resolution that night was to let go of all self-condemnation and self-rejection. It was the final lesson that life had taught him. It is the last entry because that night he died in his sleep. His journey ended with self-acceptance and self-love.

This is the true completion of the journey—loving oneself in great humility. Somehow in our brokenness, we believe that humility is to be found in self-rejection—putting down and trampling on oneself and denying one's giftedness instead of looking at and accepting one's own goodness, even as the struggle to be faithful continues. Actually, the greatest pride is self-rejection—refusing love when God has already given it. It puts one at odds with God. God loves, accepts, forgives and shows mercy. Who am I that cannot? The greatest humility is that in the face of all our mistakes and failings, hurt and pain, we can love and accept ourselves. Humility is to see ourselves as beautiful, good, holy and loving. Even though incomplete and imperfect, each of us radiates the image and likeness of God and reflects His glory.

This is the way to inner peace. It is also the gateway to true love for one's enemy, to the point of being able to say to the other: "You may be a miserable person, a sinner and a failure. I also see your humanity and goodness and I love you". No one can do that with others until it is done within one's own heart. If we can look at ourselves and see both all that is dark and all that is beautiful and good and still love our self, then we can look at another person, however vile, and do the same. We can see mistakes, failure and sin in another, but we can also see the beauty. We learn to do it first with ourselves, and then we project it outward. To love one's self is the gateway to true mercy for others. If we can love ourselves with our sin, we can love others with their sin. We know our own sin; we must guess at the state of the other's heart. We can understand something of the true mercy of God when we recall that God, who certainly knows the darkness and sin of the heart, still loves us. This is mercy: forgiveness that is not merited. God looks at us and sees the beauty and holiness in us as His people. He sees His image and loves what He sees.

If we can say "I love God" and "I believe in Jesus Christ, Son of God", God lives in our heart. To be able to see that spark of God's light within is really the gateway to life. It is the source of joy, inner peace, serenity and tranquility. We love what God loves, see what God sees, and accept what God accepts.

There is an inner beauty of the human heart that love uncovers and humility embraces. To forgive self and rejoice in God's love is true holiness in human wholeness. "I rejoice in God my Savior. He who is mighty has done good things for me" (Lk 1:47).

# Chapter 3

## *Forgiveness and the Eucharist*

The decision to forgive is often reached after much struggle. The problem with forgiveness is that there is something to forgive—hurt. Those who have never been hurt have no need to learn of forgiveness. Hurt and forgiveness belong together as a necessary pair. Forgiveness is the Christian response to hurt.

Forgiving an injury, pardoning a wrong, letting go of a hurt unjustly inflicted, are all spiritual actions that can be wrung from the depths of the soul. The work of forgiveness is not something to be taken lightly. It is never glib; it must always come from the heart. To forgive too easily or too quickly can be an escape from the real soul struggle that is the price of forgiving. Facing the pain, confronting the situation with honesty, and choosing the path of forgiveness are real works that engage the heart and soul.

The struggle ultimately is always a spiritual one and should be done in prayer. Christ Himself went into prayer in His struggles, as we see in the Agony in the Garden. His example is for our instruction and encouragement. First, we see that the decisions we make are always centered on the Father's will. Secondly, we see that making this choice can involve the agony of a spiritual battle within the soul.

It is always necessary to bring the struggle to prayer and, in the prayer, to struggle with the Father's will just as Jesus did. Certainly there are other levels of emotions, memories and feelings that are involved. These will be engaged as well. However, the most basic level of the struggle, like the decision itself, is spiritual.

Jesus is no stranger to the human struggle. He led the way by His suffering and Cross. Jesus is the man of suffering who experienced every level of hurt, injustice, betrayal, abandonment and rejection. Although deeply wounded and profoundly hurt, He won His victory through forgiveness and love. His heart was so cushioned by love, understanding, and compassion that poison from the wounds never festered so as to embitter Him or destroy Him.

His forgiveness returned love whenever injury was received. This is the spiritual victory taught by Jesus, but often beyond our reach. We need to stretch ourselves with a love that lies beyond our capacity. We find our strength in the Cross and suffering of Jesus. When we unite to the Cross in our own suffering, we also experience the victory of the Cross. Jesus suffered and died so that sins might be forgiven. It is this victory of forgiveness that we want to taste in our own lives. To unite to the Cross is to find healing in the very act of mercy.

The perfect prayer that the Lord has given us is the Eucharist. All of our spirituality flows from the Eucharist and returns there as well. It is the highest form of union with the Lord Jesus Christ. We know that the Lord Jesus is truly and fully present in the Eucharist. We know, too, that celebrating the Mass is the memorial of Jesus' Passion. The Mass is the unbloody sacrifice of Calvary rendered present in every time and place. When we celebrate the Eucharist, ". . . we proclaim the death of the Lord", St. Paul says.

The Eucharist, with its many dimensions, brings us to Calvary where we enter into Christ's Passion, are touched by it, and are united to the Sacrifice of the Cross. When the Eucharist is appreciated as a sacrifice, and celebrated authentically, each person who participates is invited to offer his or her life in, along with and through Jesus. One's life involves all the struggles, hurts, needs, feelings and emotions that make up life. It is not simply the virtues, gifts and blessings that we offer, but our basic humanity in all its frailty. That is the part of us that is still unfinished and has its share of shadows and dark corners. We offer ourselves just as we are.

When we offer ourselves to the Father in union with Jesus, we seek the pure surrender of faith that characterized His self-offering on the Cross. We offer this Eucharistic sacrifice frequently because we need to grow, mature, and deepen in that faith surrender.

At the Offertory of the Mass, bread and wine are offered to the Father. These gifts symbolize the life of each one who is sharing in the sacrifice that is being offered. They are not simply external symbols being lifted up in a devotional way. Each person is being offered. To participate means to join in personally by offering one's own heart on the altar.

The bread and wine, food and drink, symbolize life itself. We even call bread "the Staff of Life". Going more deeply into the symbolism, we recognize that these common elements have rich meaning. The bread is made from many grains of wheat, the wine from many grapes. To produce bread and wine, both wheat and grapes must be crushed and broken. Life is like that. Each life comes with a history of crushing and bruising experiences. Bread and wine symbolize not simply life in the abstract, but life with all its bruising, crushing, and painful experiences. Every person offering the Eucharist has a share in the pain of life with all its hurtful dimensions. It is these experiences that produce the need to forgive so much, so deeply, and so often. Therefore, before we reach for forgiveness, we offer our lives to the Father in union with the broken and suffering Jesus, the Crucified. The Offertory of the Mass takes on deeper meaning and becomes a healing moment. There we surrender our brokenness, painful memories, and hurts. These are let go, identified with the crushed grapes and broken wheat being offered on the altar at the hands of the priest. As we offer our lives in faith, we offer our need for healing and our desire to forgive.

At the Consecration, the bread and wine become the Body and Blood of Jesus, the Crucified One. Since we already have identified with the bread and wine, we too are taken up, consecrated, and so become the Body of Christ.

Jesus is claiming each person as His very own. What you do to this one, you do it to me because we are one, He is saying. Being one with Him and being united to Him is the healing grace. Our hurts and wounds have become His. He takes our wounds and cleanses the poison of resentment and anger. He imparts the Holy Spirit, given "for the forgiveness of sin", and pours out His redeeming blood shed for forgiveness and reconciliation. Now the flow of forgiveness is no longer ours alone, it is His.

This is Jesus—forgiving, reconciling, and embracing all in unity. It is even Jesus excusing with understanding and compassion: ". . . they know not what they do". In His heart, He holds all His people, both the hurting and the ones who inflict the hurt. He understands, more deeply than we ever will, why people hurt others. His love embraces everyone in unity and in peace. When we receive Communion, we enter into that Heart of Charity where all are reconciled and united by love and forgiveness. To be divided by anger or resentment is to negate the meaning of Communion and render it void.

To take Communion is to enter intimately into Christ Jesus and become one with Him in a profound and sacred union. As we stand in that holy place, we are linked with all those who are held in the Heart of Christ. This is the meaning of the phrase that we are the Body of Christ as Church and community. In Him there are no distinctions or barriers, no divisions, and no disunity. His mercy embraces all in equal measure of love. The Eucharist invites us to deep forgiveness in the secret places of the heart. It will never allow hidden anger or unresolved resentment to divide the Body and tear at the seamless garment of His love.

As the Eucharist invites us to that level of forgiveness and mercy, it also empowers us to achieve it. Sin is forgiven in the Sacrifice of Calvary - the very sacrifice we celebrate. The blood of Christ is poured out for pardon and reconciliation—the very blood we take at Eucharist. We are invited to place in the chalice all unforgiveness, as well as all our unhealed hurts, unmet needs, and conflicts. We cannot trust in our own strength, which is insufficient. We dare not rely on our feeble human efforts. Our hope is in Christ Jesus and the power of His perfect gift.

One of the final actions of the Mass is the thanksgiving after Communion. This is the time to rest in His Heart and absorb the gentle, yet profound, power of His love. It is the time to express gratitude and simply be thankful for saving grace.

We need to celebrate the Eucharist in a meaningful way, surrendering the need for healing, sincerely desiring a forgiving heart and choosing the path of mercy. We can then conclude the Eucharist with the final spoken prayers of gratitude and praise: "Thanks be to God!". We have touched grace and have been touched by mercy.

The Eucharist is the gift of the Father who reconciles all to Himself. It is the gift of Jesus who shares His mercy and forgiveness. It is our gift to each other in granting pardon and seeking unity as the fruit of mercy. Freely received, mercy is freely given.

"Blessed are the merciful, for mercy will be shown to them" (Matt. 5:7).

# Chapter 4

# *Forgiveness in the New Testament*

F orgiveness is an essential element of the Gospel message. It is a theme that is woven throughout the entire New Testament, with great emphasis on the importance of forgiveness as a gift that is both received from the Lord and shared with others. Each of the biblical writers speaks of forgiveness and each one does it in a distinctive way. All the New Testament authors agree that forgiveness is at the heart of all that is Christian, both in respect to what is believed in faith and what needs to be lived in practice.

The three great traditions in the New Testament are the Synoptics (Matthew, Mark and Luke), Paul in his epistles, and finally John who wrote three epistles in addition to the Gospel that bears his name. Each writer had a specific theological framework; each was living in a different situation and writing at a different time in the history of the early Church. Because of this, each writer had a unique way of speaking about Christ and also about the message of pardon, mercy and forgiveness at the heart of the Gospel. Even though each author had a different approach and language, they all placed an emphasis on forgiveness and saw it as an essential element of Christianity and one's spiritual life.

Forgiveness is the necessary link between faith and practice. Christ came for the forgiveness of sin; He graced the world with mercy. Mercy and forgiveness are neither merited nor deserved, but are free gifts. Therefore no Christian can be worthy of that name while harboring unforgiving attitudes and anger in the heart. Those who have been blessed with mercy cannot then be merciless in dealing with others. Christ has won the complete forgiveness of sin; this is grace, a free gift from God in Jesus. The grace we receive in being forgiven is exactly what we are to share in being forgiving. This is the fundamental truth when we speak of the Gospel of Jesus, and it is the cornerstone of the life of faith as well the moral life.

## Paul

Paul had his own sad struggles with Christ and a personal reason to speak of forgiveness and pardon. Paul had memories of his history before he came to terms with Christ. He would always carry these memories heavily because he had to live with what he had done at a time when he was not yet a convert. He was an ardent Jew whose world was threatened by this new sect of Christians, and as such, did everything to destroy this new community of believers in Jesus. Paul was a party to the stoning of St. Stephen. We can wonder whether Stephen's dying words, "Hold not this sin against them", touched something deep in Paul. Certainly he was confronted with a different response to adversity and persecution than anything he would have previously experienced.

Nothing in Paul's past, his education, theology, culture, or in his personal experience would have prepared him for what he witnessed that day. Stephen died without a hint of anger, self-pity or the desire for revenge. Stephen was a model of this new teaching about Jesus and for the new spirituality of Christianity. On the other hand, Paul was a model of another approach to being rejected and persecuted: anger and rage. His response to Christianity, which he saw as a threat, was completely negative. Paul was filled with murderous rage, the Scriptures tell us. Up to this point he seems to have dedicated his life to revenge and destruction in a misplaced zeal for God. He was driven by hate. There was no place in his heart, or in his theology, or in his understanding of God, for mercy, tolerance, patience or forgiveness. These would have been considered weakness by him. What was perplexing to Paul was that he had witnessed exceptional strength in Stephen. It was a stark contrast and a profound challenge for him. Paul represents the theology of chastisement without mercy and the destruction of all who are seen as the enemy—which he perceived as a service to God.

Stephen represents a theology of mercy; he forgave his enemies. While Paul lashed out with anger and destruction, Stephen reached out with love. These are two very different approaches to threats, persecution and adversity.

Then, in a moment of sheer grace, Paul encounters Christ on the road to Damascus. There he experiences the power of a love he had never known. There is no condemnation in Christ, no accusation. Just the question: "Why do you persecute me?". In this encounter we have the seeds of the theology that Paul will spend his life unfolding and teaching. He understands that in Christ Jesus there is no condemnation (Rom. 8:1). All forgiveness is grace: a gift that is undeserved and unmerited. The Father is merciful and compassionate, understanding and kind.

He is full of love for each and every person, sinners included. God has no favorites and loves each, male and female, Jew and Greek, slave and free. There is no advantage in anything external such as social standing, education, race or ethnic origin. God's forgiveness is simply given as a gift without measure.

Paul realizes full well that he was deserving of condemnation and punishment for his treatment of the Christians, yet he receives mercy. He was totally misguided in his intentions and actions, but receives only compassion and understanding. While he was hard of heart and had a closed mind, God did not hold it against him. He was a sinner but is actually redeemed and forgiven. The theology of St. Paul is the theology of grace. It is his own personal experience that taught him this. Paul understood from his encounter with Christ that faith, conversion and redemption are all gifts from God. It is all gift and can never be deserved, achieved or earned. This is the consistent teaching of Paul in his epistles—repeated often and restated in many different ways. This is his primary message: we are saved by grace! It is all gift! God is rich in mercy and loves the sinner. He offers forgiveness and pardon. For Paul, this is personal experience more than it is theology. His theology and teaching explain what he has experienced in his encounter with Christ. His conversion is a response to love; his reconciliation is a response to an invitation to relationship with the Lord.

The second insight he received in his encounter with the Lord Jesus was a strong appreciation of the Church as the Body of Christ. Christ asked: "Why do you persecute **me**?". He does not say "my people" or "my church", but **me**. There is no distinction to be made between Christ and the Christian. He lives in them, and they live in Him. The conclusion is that Christians share but one life in one Spirit. They are parts of Christ and therefore they are parts of one another. We do not exist apart from Christ and we do not exist apart from one another. The Church is the Body of Christ, each member having a different place, role and function in that Body, but still sharing in the one life of Christ.

The understanding that Paul had of the Church (as being one Body with but one Spirit) led him to insist that nothing separate or divide the community. Being united in Christ means that the Church must be one, whole and united if it is to be what it was always meant to be. In ministry and in prayer, the Church functions as an organism, with each part adding its own strength and making its unique contribution to the working of the whole body. Dissension and rivalry, competition and resentment, anger and envy all work against the Church as the Body of Christ, sap its energy, and hinder the advancement of its mission. Unity is essential and must be maintained as the highest priority for the community.

Therefore, in his epistles Paul provides both teaching and practical advice on forgiveness and pardon. Unity is maintained by active and consistent forgiveness. The one who loves "keeps no memory of wrongdoing". He exhorts the Christians to "forgive each other whenever a quarrel begins", to "do everything to maintain unity", and to "have one heart and one mind". There can be this kind of peace only when there is pardon. So the exhortation to all is "... to forgive, just as you have been forgiven". This is Paul speaking from personal experience, not theory. Love for one another, sharing in a community united in the Spirit of Christ, and being strong in the faith by having a personal relationship with Christ means that forgiveness must flow from the heart and have no measure. Just as forgiveness flows from the heart of Christ without measure, so the Christian is to live in imitation of that mystery. This is what Paul witnessed at the death of Stephen: Christ forgave sins. Stephen, the Christian, forgave sins. It is a dynamic flow of the Spirit from one to the other.

If the Christian is forgiven, then there must be forgiveness as the ultimate hallmark of a life lived in faith. First, it is the only way to be authentic as one who has received forgiveness. What is received must be shared, not hoarded. Then, if we are one in the Body of Christ, maintaining unity must be held as the highest priority. And unity can never be maintained without constant and heartfelt forgiveness. Paul would warn anyone who would tear apart the community that this, in fact, is to destroy the temple of God and desecrate it. Forgiveness is a response to being forgiven and a necessary component for a life shared with others in the Church.

The example and teaching of Jesus are not theories, but living realities with practical consequences. This would be St. Paul's understanding of the gift of mercy. His experience was too real to be ignored or dismissed. He received mercy from the infinite riches of God in Jesus. Everyone can and should and, in fact, have received mercy as grace and gift.

**John**

Another author of the New Testament is St. John, who wrote not only the Gospel that bears his name, but three letters and the Book of Revelation as well. Leaving aside the Book of Revelation which deals with things apocalyptic, we have John's understanding of

Jesus, His word and message recorded both in the Gospel and in his letters to the community. Here we find a different language, voice and tone in the telling of the Gospel story. There is a unique style and emphasis in John's story of Jesus. Instead of the theological reflections and blunt language of Paul, John is much more mystical and reflective. John's writings positively soar. His writings are simpler, more spiritual, and somewhat more cryptic. But it is the same message and the same core truth. Since John has a different history and experience with Jesus, this brings him to reflect differently in his Gospel.

John was a disciple of Jesus. He was with the Lord and had a relationship with Him that would be the envy of anyone. As one of the Twelve, John was a witness to the miracles, healings and signs that Jesus performed. As one of the Twelve, he heard all of the teachings firsthand and had even deeper conversations with the Lord where the teachings were explained. Even beyond all this, John had something special. He was called the "Beloved Disciple" because of his unique and close relationship with Jesus. John sat next to Jesus at the last supper and leaned his head on Jesus' chest. John was the only apostle at the foot of the cross, and there he was entrusted with Mary the mother of Jesus. John brought Mary into his home and had a mother and son relationship with her. It was that same disciple, John, who was a witness to the transfiguration, the agony in the garden, and the appearances of the Risen Lord. He holds a unique place in the Gospel story as a witness and guide to the inner depth of the Gospel message.

John went on to live a long life and had time to reflect and meditate on the word and work of Jesus. What he wrote in his Gospel and letters comes from a

deep place of reflection and prayer. There is nothing
superfluous in his writings, just the essence and heart of
the message. He soars to mystical heights, but always
remains rooted in the Jesus he knew.

What is important to John is the gift of love that he
discovered in Jesus. Love is at the heart of the Gospel
and the key to understanding everything there is to
know about Jesus. Along with love comes the gift of
mercy and forgiveness that is the essence of His work.
Jesus came, sent by the Father as a gift of love: "God so
loved the world that He sent His only begotten Son"
(John 3:16).

Jesus tells us that He did not come for
condemnation, but for forgiveness and reconciliation: "I
did not come to condemn the world" (John 3:17). In a
story told only by John, the woman caught committing
adultery is sent away with the words: "I will not
condemn you; now go in peace". This story captures
the whole ministry of Jesus and His gift of love. He
came not to punish, chastise or accuse, but to redeem.
Although obviously a sinner, she is forgiven and
accepted and loved.

Toward the end of his life, after much experience
with community and preaching the Gospel, John writes
letters to the communities with which he was
associated. Three of these letters are preserved for us in
the New Testament and as such are to be considered
inspired and normative.

These letters, written after a lifetime of prayer,
contemplation and experience, capture the essence of the
Gospel message. Here we find John's focus on what he
considers most important about Christ. It is here that he
reminds the community: "God *is* love". This is a
hallmark of truth for anyone who wants to live in God,

to be a follower of Christ: it is the mark of love. It is not possible to be a follower of Christ and harbor hate in the heart. No Christian can proclaim love of God and have a heart closed to love of others. God is light. His love is a light. Hate is darkness and an evil. Light and darkness cannot coexist in the heart. Love and unforgiveness contradict one another.

In language that is mystical as well as simple and plain spoken, John reminds us that in God and in the light of His love there is no place for the darkness of hate, revenge or division. Only love can stand before the pure light of God's love that shines *on* the believer as well as *in* the believer.

All that is unlovely and unloving must be purged from the Christian's heart. The light of love, which is God, cannot coexist with the darkness of hate and resentment. Forgiveness is the language that love speaks and the only language that God wants to hear, for that is the language that He speaks to us in His Son Jesus.

To claim fellowship with Jesus and not have love is to be a liar, saying with the lips what is denied in the heart. Behavior contradicts what the words profess when there is even a hint of hate, prejudice, bigotry, unforgiveness, anger or revenge in the heart. The Christian standard is indeed a high one; the gift of mercy given in Jesus is indeed exalted as well. John reflects on the gift that is given in Jesus—the Father's unconditional love and mercy—and then draws the logical conclusion that all who receive this grace from God must reflect the light of that love.

John, for all his mysticism and his soaring to heights of spiritual contemplation, comes back to the very human, mundane reality of forgiveness as the necessary gift in all relationships. Relationships to the community and to enemies need to be gauged by the measure of love. The relationship to God is gauged the same way. Only what is authentically loving can be authentically Christian and of God. There are not two realities or two worlds—a spiritual one of God and an earthly one of sinners. There is one reality, and it is all of God. It is His light that shines on us all and brings us into the heart of mercy where we discover one another in a fellowship of love. It is the gift that is given and shared that is the cornerstone of all spirituality. Prayer and spirituality are not escapes from relationship, but rather draw us to true and authentic community based on the love of God at the heart of all relationships.

John understood Christ as perhaps no one else ever has. He glimpsed the depths of Jesus' heart and experienced for himself the overwhelming love at its center. He was lifted to exalted heights and knew the ecstasy of spiritual union with His Beloved. He was plunged into the ocean of God's love and was given deep insights into Jesus' glory and His relationship to the Father. He experienced the mystery of a love that cannot be expressed in human words. He was almost blinded by the light of God's glory. John was privileged beyond the other disciples and greatly graced. He is well called the Beloved Disciple.

In the first chapter of John's Gospel, he tells us that "no one has ever seen God", but it is the one closest to the heart of God, Jesus, who has made Him known. Toward the end of the Gospel, at the last supper, we encounter John leaning on Jesus' chest. He is there identified as one who is closest to the heart of Jesus and can therefore make Him known.

We listen intently and with great interest when John speaks of the essence of the mystery he tried so hard to communicate. It is, in the end, of breathtaking simplicity. God is love, and to live in God is to live in love. John knew the truth of love, taught from the heart of Jesus to his own heart.

## The Synoptics

The "Synoptic Gospels" is a term used for the three Gospels written by Mark, Luke and Matthew. Just as John has a style all his own, so these three, even as each has a uniqueness all his own, share a common language, approach and style. As such, they are usually clustered together. These three are the storytellers of the New Testament. We find here neither the theological sophistication of Paul nor the mysticism of John. In the Synoptics, we do find the story of Jesus told as it was remembered, preached and shared by the contemporaries of Jesus. It is the Gospel story in human terms for all to hear. These three Gospels are replete with stories of healings and miracles, along with the parable stories, the teachings of Jesus, and remembrances of various events in His life. They tell of His travels and the meals He shared at the homes of friend and foe alike. There are also the human touches in the Gospels such as Jesus' relationship with His disciples, the controversies with the elders and Pharisees, the journeys and the crowds that followed Him, as well as the times He sought rest and prayer away from the crowds.

The Synoptic Gospels are the records of the earliest preaching in the Church as the Apostles began to share the story of Jesus with the larger world. The language is simple and direct, the message clear and straightforward.

The teachings of Jesus do not seem to be deep theology at first glance (although they lend themselves to theologizing) because of their simplicity. He taught simple truths and spoke of the Father and His love, mercy and forgiveness. He told parables to paint a picture of the Father, as in the stories of the Prodigal Son and the Good Shepherd. His commands for living a moral life are likewise simple and direct, and all are based on an understanding of the Father's love. If the Father forgives, so must we forgive. If the Father has compassion, so His children must show compassion. If the Father is merciful, so the ones who have benefited from His mercy must likewise be merciful to others.

Again, Jesus uses simple language and word pictures to drive home the teaching. He tells us that it is more important to leave the sacrifice unoffered in order to reconcile with someone who has been offended. It is important to be united in heart and spirit when praying, and therefore, forgiveness must be a daily exercise. The story of Jesus told in such a human way would necessarily emphasize the need for forgiveness. In the Gospels, we read of the reality of life shared in community with the attendant need to forgive many times over. Relationships are not idealized, but are honestly presented. The apostles will argue about who is the greatest and who will get the favored positions. The fact that they argue at all shows a human face to the gathering of disciples. Peter, who has been listening to teaching after teaching on forgiveness, will cry out in exasperation: "How many times am I supposed to forgive?".

Indeed, forgiveness is as difficult as it is necessary. The Synoptic Gospels know the reality of daily life, relationships and community. That is one reason there is an emphasis on forgiving as an essential component to the life of the Church. Only forgiveness and pardon will enable the Church to be in unity, as well as the individual Christian to be faithful to the heart of the Gospel. For the Synoptics, forgiveness is the lifeblood of the community of disciples. If John puts the stress on the gift of love, especially in his letters, the Synoptics put the emphasis on the gift of mercy and forgiveness. In the Gospels of Matthew, Mark and Luke, Jesus speaks about forgiveness more than any other single topic. Less mystical and less romantic than love, forgiveness is however the realistic and necessary virtue for the Church's life and survival. Love is the ideal; forgiveness is its expression. Love is the goal to attain; forgiveness is the daily journey of a life shared with others in the Church.

## New Testament

The thread of forgiveness weaves its way through the entire New Testament, constituting essentially the very fabric of the Gospel. It is expressed in teaching and command, story and parable, warning and exhortation. Forgiveness is the foundation, necessary for any understanding of the mission and identity of Jesus. Sometimes theologians who choose to focus on other matters put it into the background. At other times it is all but ignored as perhaps too obvious and self-evident. Or it may be thought too mundane, too human, or maybe too challenging for serious prayer and reflection. The fact remains that the gift of mercy and forgiveness is not just the message of the Gospel—it *is* the Gospel.

Redemption, salvation, the Cross, and the Resurrection are all about the gift of mercy and forgiveness freely given by the Father in Jesus Christ. It is the very purpose and reason for the Incarnation. Jesus is the Father's atoning gift offered to the world so that sin may be forgiven. In the words of John the Baptist, Jesus is the Lamb of God who takes away the sins of the world. It is Jesus' deepest identity.

Forgiveness and mercy are in essence the new commandment called love. It is a *new* command because this love is not to be restricted to friend and benefactor. The love called for by this new commandment is broad, wide and deep. It is universal and all embracing. Love for one's enemy can only happen when the enemy is forgiven. Otherwise, love is an empty shell, something without real substance or content, a very human response to being loved by loving in return. Christ called for love of enemy and foe, the grateful and ungrateful, friend and enemy alike. This is a novel teaching and stretches the human heart to new dimensions of love.

This is possible because we are first loved and forgiven without condition or restriction. What is received as gift is to be given as gift. What is received without cost is to be given without payment.

Be compassionate as your heavenly Father is compassionate. He lets the rain fall and the sun shine on the good and the bad, the just and the unjust. Do not judge who is worthy and who is not, who is deserving and who is not. Be perfect as your heavenly Father is perfect. Love and do not count the cost. Forgive as you have been forgiven. You have been shown mercy, now show mercy.

In this is the whole of the Gospel of Jesus Christ.

# Chapter 5

## *Forgiveness in the Old Testament The Story of Joseph*

The Old Testament lays the groundwork for the Gospel of Jesus Christ. It has much to say about love, forgiveness and reconciliation. The Hebrew Scriptures have deep and touching insights into human behavior, motivation and personal relationships. There is much to learn from the stories of the Old Testament which are touchingly human and quite realistic when it comes to putting a mirror up to the human drama of life. The stories entertain on one level, while at the same time they edify and teach deep truths.

The Book of Genesis is a series of stories about human struggle, about the drama of relationships and the difficulties encountered in trying to find meaning and balance in daily life. In the Genesis stories people interact, compete for power and honor, and hurt each other along the way. Forgiveness as well as unforgiveness, anger, resentment and revenge would be the overriding themes of Genesis. The need for reconciliation and how to attain it would ultimately be the lessons taught in the Book of Genesis.

First of all, it is important to see Genesis as a book in its own right. It is the first book of the Bible, which is a collection of books. As a book, Genesis has a beginning and an end, a theme and a lesson. It is a collection of stories that tie together as a single story unfolding with drama and with much spiritual insight. The teaching of the book is rightly considered to be God's Word to the world. Genesis, as much as any other book of the Bible, is to be accepted as divine revelation and inspired by the Holy Spirit. Its method is to tell stories and in the stories themselves will be found life-giving teaching, revelation and all the wisdom of God's Word.

The most common word in the Book of Genesis (other than an obvious one like *God*) is the word *struggle*. The theme of the whole Book of Genesis is the need to be in human relationships and the constant discord and the shattering of relationships through misunderstanding, anger, jealousy, envy, competition and everything else that plagues the human condition. Every story, one after another, is about the pain of broken relationships and the struggle to find some degree of unity and harmony within the human family. Cain and Abel, Abraham and Lot, Isaac and Ishmael, Jacob and Esau, Sarah and Hagar, Rachael and Leah, Jacob and Laban, as well as myriad others, are stories of struggle with relationship. They compete, they vie, and they struggle with and against each other. In every case, the outcome is not happy. The only solution to the struggles in relationship seems to be to separate and end the relationship, or else live in an uneasy and uncomfortable truce. Most often separation in some way or another is the only outcome.

Cain kills Abel, Jacob runs away from Esau, Sarah banishes Hagar and Ishmael, Jacob separates from Laban. It all seems to be summed up in the words of Abraham who solves a problem of conflict with Lot. He tells Lot to choose: "If you go east, I will go west, and if you go west, I will go east". He recognized that they could no longer live together. Rather than unity or reconciliation, they needed to put space and distance between them and go their separate ways. That is the only solution that Abraham could foresee and the only way he could find to move beyond discord into peace.

There is no happy outcome in any of the Genesis stories, just separation and the severing of relationship as if that is the only way that people could maintain a civil society. There is a winner and a loser every time, but no resolution, no reconciliation, no unity. It is in this context that we read the story of Joseph and his brothers.

The Book of Genesis concludes with the well known story of Joseph and his brothers. As a story, it takes up the bulk of Genesis. Over thirty percent of the entire Book of Genesis is given over to this one story. It is meant to be the conclusion to the Book of Genesis and to contain the insight and answer to the problem of human relationships that always seem to break beyond repair.

The story of Joseph is well known. Jacob has twelve sons and Joseph is by far the favored one. To him is given the famous coat of many colors. He is a man who dreams of future glory and seems to be a favorite of God, as well as his father Jacob. As in the rest of the book of Genesis, the theme of the Joseph story is a struggle in relationships, this time between Joseph and his brothers. It is strife that is caused by jealousy and envy, as in so many of the other Genesis stories. Joseph's brothers betray him, attempt to kill him and eventually sell him into slavery. It is betrayal and rejection in the extreme, a violation of family and of brotherhood. The actions of the brothers towards Joseph are heartless and cruel. Any relationship between

Joseph and his brothers seems to end in bitterness, sin and tragedy. It is another sad tale of brokenness, hurt and pain. It is a dark tale, perhaps the darkest of any of the Genesis stories.

Joseph, sold into slavery, ends up in Egypt and ultimately succeeds to move beyond his state of slavery, by God's blessing and grace. He is raised up to high office at the right hand of the Pharaoh. Joseph is a wise and gifted leader who manages the affairs of Egypt with great prudence. Because of Joseph's foresight, the Egyptians store up grain against an impending famine so that when the famine strikes the land, the country and its people are secure, and other people come from far and wide to buy grain from the Egyptians. So it is that the stage is set for the brothers of Joseph to travel to Egypt and encounter Joseph again after many years. Jewish tradition has it that Joseph had been in Egypt well over thirty years when the brothers came calling.

There are three scenes in the story that are worth considering for our purpose here. Each scene speaks to us of forgiveness, healing and reconciliation, something not found in any other story in Genesis. Each scene involves an abundance of tears that speak of the depth of emotion involved in the story. The stories teach us about the power of forgiveness, the healing that comes from pardoning, and the path to reconciliation. Genesis will end with a story like its other stories in that it involves struggle and discord in relationships with the accustomed separation. But it also involves healing and reconciliation, something that is notably missing from any other story in Genesis. Forgiveness makes the difference. It produces a happy ending. Division is replaced with unity at long last because there is a way to reconciliation. This is ultimately the lesson of the whole

Book of Genesis: forgiveness is the key to relationships and is necessary to unity and peace.

The first of the scenes is when the brothers come down to Egypt to buy grain during the famine. (This part of the story can be read in chapter 42 of Genesis). They come for grain, but they encounter Joseph. He recognizes them, but they do not recognize him so they have no idea that they are speaking to the brother that they had betrayed so long ago. Joseph toys with them and accuses them of being spies and announces that he wants to arrest them. Certainly, on a human level, Joseph is playing with their emotions and is taking a bit of revenge on them. After all, he is still carrying the wounds of their betrayal and rejection. Joseph's accusations cause fear and consternation among the brothers. Immediately they decide that their misfortune is due to their sin against Joseph. This shows the power of guilt. Over thirty years have passed, but when misfortune strikes, they immediately remember their sin of long ago and still fear its consequences.

Unabsolved sin lives on in the spirit and still has power over the mind and heart. Guilt is a powerful emotion when it is carried in the heart without resolution. It is a weight that does not grow lighter with the passing years. Guilt lives on in the human spirit and needs to encounter truth and forgiveness if it is to find resolution. Since the brothers had neither, their guilt was a living reality that weighed on their hearts.

For Joseph, this is a moment of catharsis. The brothers are speaking Hebrew and are unaware that Joseph understands what they are saying. They are speaking about him and the terrible things they did to him so long ago. As Joseph listens to them, all the feelings he has carried in his heart these many years suddenly surface and break through to his conscious mind. He loses his composure and begins to weep. He turns away from them so that they will not see his tears. He is not ready to face them or to deal with the hurt they caused him. He has carried the pain and has kept it buried inside for too long. I suppose that we could say in today's language that "he needed time".

We understand well that the betrayal and rejection that Joseph endured were still felt deep in his soul. Like guilt, hurts live on in the deep places of the spirit until healed or resolved. Joseph may have been able to continue on with his life and deal with these feelings on some level, but they were never resolved. The feelings and emotions, the memories and hurts, were perhaps well buried, but nothing was ever healed in his heart. Now it all surfaces and comes out in a flood of tears. It is the hurt, sorrow, pain and heartache, anger and rage, self-pity, the desire to retaliate – they have been carried all this time in a wounded heart. These things remained alive within him and needed to surface and to be faced. All that was buried in his heart now surfaces in an outburst of emotion. The hurts are real, the emotions are real, and Joseph needs to deal with them. Denial and avoidance no longer work.

So the first lesson that the Joseph story teaches is about honesty in dealing with all of the hurts of the past and the need to deal with the wounds that have been inflicted over the years. Carrying them without awareness produces a bitter heart and not a few neuroses. Facing them honestly and dealing with them with integrity may involve a struggle and some tears, but there is no other way to proceed to healing and reconciliation.

The next scene teaches about the power of love and forgiveness. (This part of the story can be read in chapter 45 of Genesis.)

The brothers return to buy more grain since the famine continues to afflict the region. This time when they come, they bring Benjamin with them, as Joseph had demanded. Benjamin, among all the brothers, is the only one who is Joseph's full brother. When Joseph sees all his brothers, this time with Benjamin, he again breaks down in tears. They have all been reunited. It must have been for Joseph an answer to many prayers. He has his whole family back with him. He may have been successful, rich and famous in Egypt but there was still an empty place in his heart – he did not have his family. Now he has all the brothers together with him, including his favorite, Benjamin. He weeps uncontrollably and reveals himself to the brothers: "It is I, Joseph, your brother. The one you sold into slavery". There proceeds to unfold a scene of tenderness and affection, with tears and embraces, as the brothers reunite after so long a time. Included in the reunion is reconciliation and pardon. Only forgiveness makes this reunion possible. It is the centerpiece of the tale.

We find here the scene of Joseph forgiving his brothers for what they had done to him and absolving them from guilt: "Do not be angry with yourselves for what you have done to me". He reinterprets the experience as an inspired event preordained and part of the plan of God: "God sent me here ahead of you". Certainly it is the gift of hindsight, but it gives us an understanding of his thinking, faith and prayer. God is in charge. He uses everyone and everything to accomplish His purposes. God is even more powerful than sin.

The wisdom of Joseph, born of much prayer, suffering and reflection, has found the providence of God at work, even in human tragedy, weakness and sin. God is so great and so almighty and powerful that He can even use sin and treachery to accomplish His will. His hand is in all things. So, with this understanding, Joseph forgives and absolves the brothers for what they had done. There are many tears shed, and for several reasons. Joseph is weeping in gratitude for the reuniting of his family. The brothers are weeping in relief for the absolution and forgiveness that they are receiving, bringing freedom from the guilt that they have been carrying for all these years. All are weeping tears of forgiveness, both in the giving of it and the receiving of it. The tears are washing away a lifetime of pain and anguish. Only forgiveness can make anything different. Guilt is washed away; hurt and sorrow are cleansed from the soul; anger and resentment are healed. Joseph has forgiven them and expressed understanding and compassion for them. He offers them a home in Egypt and a haven from the poverty and the distress all around them. He welcomes them to his country. Most importantly, he welcomes them into his heart.

So the second lesson learned here is the power of forgiveness. Certainly Joseph had the option of exacting revenge, closing his heart to them, refusing to receive them and holding a grudge against his brothers. He had a right to do so, in a sense, using the standard of the world. Joseph is remembered by us today because he did not use the standard of the world. He used the heart of God as his standard. He chose to forgive them, to receive them and to let go of the past. Because he chose the path of forgiveness, the family was reunited and relationships restored. There was healing and reconciliation, unity and peace. Without forgiveness there would have been an entirely different story, if it were told at all. Without forgiveness it would have been the same story as the all others, of continuing strife and division, and maybe revenge, rather than resolution and reunion. As a family, they are reborn and can have a new beginning.

Forgiveness made all the difference.

The last scene to focus on, for our purpose here, is the last chapter of the Book of Genesis. (This scene can be found in chapter 50 of the Book of Genesis.) The brothers have been living in Egypt for 17 years when Jacob, their father, dies. The brothers, still not secure in the forgiveness of Joseph, fear that he might turn on them now that their father is dead. So they go to him as a group to plead with him. This is the last scene in the Book of Genesis. In a sense, it is the conclusion, not just to the Joseph story, but to the whole Book of Genesis. The brothers finally speak the words they should have spoken many years before but did not. They say to Joseph: "Please forgive the sins and the wrongs that we committed against you. We are sorry for treating you so badly. We were wrong". They were admitting their guilt and taking responsibility for their behavior. They were humbly asking for pardon and apologizing for all the pain and heartbreak they caused.

And again, Joseph weeps. Hearing these words must have touched a place deep in his heart and released deep emotions. After the scene of forgiveness and reconciliation, what more could be added to the story of healing? It was a complete story now, with a resolution that heals and instructs and inspires down to our day.

The betrayal of Joseph had taken place more than forty-five years previous to this scene. Yet this is the first and only time that the brothers say the words that Joseph desperately needed to hear: "We are sorry - please forgive us for the wrong we did to you". Asking forgiveness is an important part of reconciliation. The story is finally completed when they can admit guilt and ask pardon.

Joseph had already forgiven without being asked. In all those years, he never accused or condemned the brothers. He waited for God's time, which certainly seemed a long time in coming. But it came. The brothers admitted their guilt and asked forgiveness. Now the reconciliation was complete.

If Joseph had waited for the brothers to admit guilt and ask forgiveness, nothing would have happened previously. No reconciliation, no healing, no reunion would have taken place without Joseph's having freely forgiven. But Joseph, in God's wisdom, showed mercy and there was reunion. He followed the lead of God and forgave freely without qualification. The family was restored. Peace was reestablished.

Then at the proper time (God's time), the brothers were able to admit guilt, take responsibility for their actions and ask forgiveness. The process can be completed. Now there is more than forgiveness, there is total reconciliation. Forgiveness was a seed that was planted and allowed to grow to maturity so as to produce the fruit of reconciliation and healing. Forgiveness in the heart of Joseph was his spirituality and the sign of true holiness. Reconciliation with the brothers is the final result of his love and brings about the gift of unity.

So the Book of Genesis ends with a story of mercy, forgiveness and reconciliation. It lays the groundwork and foreshadows the redemption that Jesus will bring: mercy, forgiveness of sin, and reconciliation.

The Scriptures speak to the deepest needs of the human heart, the most complex problems and the most difficult struggles of life. The theme of forgiveness weaves its way throughout the Bible as a consistent teaching because this is the key to unlocking the mysteries and secrets of the heart. The Word of God teaches us the way to success in life and in living. Love, life, family, and relationships are all in need of forgiveness as daily food to survive. Without forgiveness, everything worth living for withers and dies.

The story of Joseph is not just a dramatic tale of betrayal and success. It is a valuable lesson from the Scriptures that contains wisdom for life and a revelation from God. This is true spiritual life and authentic religion, with Joseph as the example and model. Endure and forgive, live and love and pardon, and find reconciliation and peace.

The heart of God is revealed to us in the Scriptures as a heart of forgiveness and mercy. It is His essence and identity – to be love and mercy, pardon and peace. We, who are created in His image, become most truly spiritual and most maturely human when we become forgiving and compassionate in the deepest possible way.

"Be compassionate, as your Father is compassionate... then it will be evident that you are truly children of the heavenly Father." (Lk: 6,36)

# Chapter 6

## *The Gift is Mercy*

F orgiveness is the key to understanding the heart
of the Christian message. It is the command, the
necessity, and the spiritual law governing all
relationships, both with God and others. Forgiveness is
the theme that weaves itself throughout the whole
Biblical story; it is the basis of all the teachings of Christ.
It is for this that He came and for this that He died – for
the forgiveness of sin. He teaches, models and lives the
message of forgiveness. It is the overriding message we
are left to ponder and live. Forgiveness is the essence
and heart of Christ and of Christianity itself.

We are forgiven. We forgive. This sums up the
essence of Christian spirituality. Followers of Christ
know the need of forgiveness and walk the path of
mercy.

The danger is that the theme of forgiveness can
become a demand to forgive, and as such, a law which
can be burdensome and difficult to obey. There are
enough commandments already without having Christ
add another one - and one that is sometimes humanly
impossible to fulfill.

At the end of this meditation of forgiveness, it is
important to leave with the emphasis on forgiveness as a
gift and a grace. Forgiveness is a grace first and a
commandment second. This is the foundation for all
thinking and praying about forgiveness: we are forgiven,

freely and undeservedly, of all our sins. It is the grace that is rightly called amazing. We have received mercy, and so understand forgiveness.

People who know their need for forgiveness appreciate and treasure this great gift. They find it easier to forgive because they have been forgiven themselves. People who are less aware of their own sin appreciate less what Christ has given to them. There are people who find their sanctification in the keeping of all the rules. Correct behavior, ritual, rubric and tradition are all important for these people and in them they find a certain satisfaction and security. These are the ones who find it more difficult to forgive others because they do not treasure the grace of forgiveness. These are the ones the Gospels call self-righteous. They were closed to Christ while sinners flocked to Him. The difference lies in the forgiveness Christ came to offer. For some, it is a breath of hope and a relief from the burden of guilt. For others it is a scandal and a stumbling block. Mercy is good news to those who hunger for it. It is a difficulty for those who feel self-satisfied and holy in their own smug world of ritual correctness.

This is the story that unfolds in the Gospel. It is important to focus on the drama because it is the essence of the Gospel and is the very identity of Christ. "His name will be called Jesus because He will save His people from their sins." Christ came for forgiveness and grants mercy freely. It is for this that He suffered rejection and, ultimately, the Cross. But it is His identity and His primary work. He forgives sin. His name is mercy. He died so that sinners could live.

There are many stories in the Gospel that teach the same lesson. Here we will focus on one that seems to gather all of the strands of the Gospel together with great clarity. It is the story of the woman caught "in the very act" of committing adultery. (This story can be found in John's Gospel, chapter 8.) There is no question of her guilt. According to the law, she must be stoned to death. Mosaic law is very clear and clean cut. The guilty deserved to die because of their sin. When they bring the adulteress to Jesus, He brings no accusation against her. Rather, He sends her away with the words: "I do not condemn you". In Christ there is no condemnation (Rom: 8.1). The story has many layers of meaning and is rich in symbols and allusions to the whole mystery and work of Jesus.

First, it is meant to contain an echo of, and be in contrast to, the story found in the Book of Daniel where a woman is unjustly accused of adultery. Daniel, a young man at the time, has the wisdom to uncover the injustice and prove her innocence. As a consequence, the woman is freed from an unjust death by stoning. God comes to the aid of the innocent who is victim to injustice.

In the New Testament story, Jesus, with astounding wisdom, saves an adulterous woman from death by stoning. The difference is that in the Old Testament, God defends and protects the innocent; in the New Testament, God defends and protects the guilty. This is a powerful and earth-shattering change in our understanding of God. There is no need to appease God, or to atone for sin, or overcome guilt by our own efforts. It cannot be done. Sin demands justice. The wages of sin is death. It is all very clear both in philosophy and in theology. If God is offended, the offence is infinite and demands retribution. In justice, we are all guilty and deserve to die, and we would die in our sins if it were not for Jesus. Sin demands atonement. That is why the Jewish religion had sacrifices. Indeed it is why many different religions have sacrifice: to atone for sin and to be a substitution for the sinner who is the one deserving of death. No amount of sacrifice can ever appease the infinite Creator. No amount of blood can atone for sin. We are left with guilt and a restless search to find peace and reconciliation. But God sends His Son to accomplish what no human can accomplish – be the pure and perfect sin offering that finally atones for sin.

Jesus Himself meets the demands of justice and dies for all. By that death on the Cross, all sinners find freedom and forgiveness. Sin is forgiven and all is made new in Christ because of the Cross and Resurrection. He is the atonement for sin, the sacrificial lamb, the ultimate sin offering. Without His sacrificial death, there is no pardon and no reconciliation with God. He came to save the human race from sin. It is His mission and identity: Jesus - "the One who saves".

We find this brought out with great clarity in the story of this sinful woman. She is brought to Jesus, guilty and deserving of death by stoning according to the Law of Moses. Jesus bends down and writes in the dirt and utters the famous words: "Let him who is without sin cast the first stone". They all depart, slipping off one by one, beginning with the eldest. Then Jesus stands up, faces the woman and tells her: "I do not condemn you. Go in peace and sin no more". Jesus forgives sin. He acquits the sinner. He absolves from guilt. He shows mercy. He **is** mercy incarnate.

So the first lesson is that Jesus forgives sin and absolves from guilt. He does not condemn, not even those worthy of condemnation.

The story deserves a closer look, at deeper layers of symbol and meaning. The first question that must be answered is how a woman who is guilty and worthy of condemnation when the story begins, is guiltless and without condemnation when the story concludes. Is there a lack of true justice here? How does it happen? What is the link, what is the important insight here that we need to understand? How are the guilty declared guiltless? Of course the fact that Jesus forgives sin is the ultimate key. But there is more to understand, and it lies in the way that sin is forgiven. How is pardon found and peace won? There is a deep theological insight into the essential identity of Jesus which we need to grasp. It is found here in symbols within the story, as in a Semitic style of teaching. Stories teach lessons. Every gesture and detail is important to consider because they contain deeper meanings than is immediately evident on the surface.

The woman is obviously guilty. She is being publicly embarrassed, shamed and humiliated as she is dragged before the crowd. The whole point of bringing her into a public arena is to embarrass and humiliate her. She deserves death because of her sin, but the leaders want to add to her torment and bring her public shame. So they bring her in quite a dramatic manner to Jesus, ready to stone her to death.

Why is she brought before Jesus? Where is His connection to her sin and condemnation? It is because the leaders are looking to trap Jesus, even as they humiliate the woman. In a way that parallels the situation of the woman, they are looking to shame and embarrass Jesus as well. So they think that they are bringing Him a question that cannot be answered and a problem that cannot be solved. As a rabbi and loyal Jew,

He cannot contradict the Mosaic law that demands her death. As one who preaches mercy and forgiveness, He cannot call for her death either. So they hope to trap Him with the situation and embarrass Him into silence.

In this, the woman and Jesus share common ground. They are both found in a situation where they are meant to be embarrassed, shamed and humiliated. Jesus takes onto Himself the condition of a sinner (though free from sin Himself) and experiences the same lot as the guilty. "For our sake, He became sin" (II Cor 5,21). Jesus does not just touch the sinner from a safe distance, but enters into the state of the sinner to share the suffering that sin brings. Like Daniel of old, Jesus will have the wisdom to confront the difficulty, answer the question, and solve the dilemma. He is not caught in the trap, but is freed from the snare set for Him. And with Him, the sinner is also set free. Our struggle is His struggle; His victory is our victory. So we have the shadow of the Cross over the story, illuminating the message of the Gospel with striking clarity.

Another thing to notice in the story is that the woman is never named. She is just a sinner, caught in her sin. The reason for not naming her is important. It is because this is a story not just about one sinner in a particular time and place, but about each and every person who has sinned and whose sin cries out for punishment and condemnation. Whether a sin is public or private, known or unknown, it deserves punishment and so every sinner deserves to suffer and die. We are to understand, therefore, that each and every one of us is that woman brought before Jesus, guilty of sin. Her story is our story, so that what happens to the woman happens to us. Her fate is ours, so we need to pay close attention to the story as it unfolds.

The outcome of the story, as we know, is that Jesus will proclaim freedom from condemnation. At this time, it is important to recognize in the unfolding of the story what it is that brings the sinner forgiveness and just how the guilty becomes guiltless.

Jesus stoops down and writes in the dirt. Then He stands up. In those gestures lies the teaching. Much attention has been brought to this act of writing, with the obvious question as to what it was that He wrote. We will never know the answer since the Scriptures do not tell us. Anything said about it is pure conjecture. The focus should be on Jesus Himself. Jesus is the Word that is written in the dirt or soil from which human flesh is made. He is God's Word and He took flesh to dwell among us and take on our sin.

First, He stooped down. He bent down, or He lowered Himself, to use a scriptural reference. This is a symbol of the Incarnation. Jesus did not deem equality with God something to cling to. Rather, He lowered Himself; He humbled Himself, to become human and take on human flesh. If the Father had scooped up the dirt and dust of the earth to fashion mankind, Jesus will lower Himself to the level of dust and dirt in order to redeem mankind. He wrote His name on the lowest and lowliest part of our nature, our flesh. All of this is symbolically included in the simple phrase that tells us that He lowered Himself and wrote in the dirt on the ground. He wrote His name on human nature and claimed it as His own. This is the Incarnation in its essence.

After lowering Himself to write on the ground, He stood up – or to be more literal, He rose up. If the bending down is symbolic of the Incarnation, the rising up is symbolic of the Resurrection. It is here that we

understand the process that makes a sinner who is
worthy of condemnation to become free of
condemnation and absolved of sin. Jesus came to earth,
became flesh, took our human nature to the Cross and
then rose again. When He rose, all creation was made
new. The old world was gone and there was a new
creation, recreated in grace and mercy. Sin found its
atonement, and forgiveness was won for all. The whole
of creation is different because Jesus became man,
suffered, died and rose from the dead. "Behold I make
all things new." (Rev: 21,5) The mercy of God is the
ultimate reality, sin is not. God's love endures and is
stronger than evil. The act of creation is astounding in
its power and majesty; the act of re-creation is
astounding in its love and mercy.

So in the Gospel story, when Jesus rises up, He can
look at the woman and truthfully tell her: "I do not
condemn you. Go in peace". She leaves that place a new
person, redeemed and literally born again. In Christ
Jesus there is no condemnation, only mercy.

So as we consider the importance of forgiveness, the
final word is not on the necessity to forgive, nor the
need to pardon injuries, as important as these are. The
first and final word is that Jesus has forgiven sin, we are
free from guilt and condemnation, and amazing grace is
found in God's overwhelming gift of mercy. Having
received such a gift, can we fail to share it or could we
ever withhold it from others? Certainly we have all
sinned and certainly we have all been sinned against.
The response to both is forgiveness, received and given.
What is received as gift is to be given as gift. The gift is
forgiveness, undeserved and without conditions; the
grace is healing and wholeness and peace. Forgiveness is
more than an act of kindness; it is a re-creation in love

of what is broken and shattered in life. Only forgiveness redeems. God in His infinite and incomprehensible love has forgiven sin in Jesus Christ, His Son. We who have received such a gift of mercy can never hesitate to share the gift of mercy.

We read the story of a woman caught in sin and finding redemption and forgiveness in Jesus. Her life was surely changed in a dramatic fashion, so that she becomes the symbol of a mercy that defies human logic. Every one of us finds an echo in her story. The sinner is forgiven and set free. There is no condemnation in Jesus Christ. Sin is atoned for when He took our sinful nature to the Cross.

The final word is mercy. There is no greater gift, no higher morality, no deeper insight. We are forgiven freely and without condition. Jesus is mercy incarnate who holds us in His arms with strong, yet tender love. In Him we are safe enough to forgive injury and insults. In Him we find the strength and grace to forgive the seemingly unforgivable. In Jesus we learn the true depth of love which forgives and pardons and grants peace. His Cross, suffering and death, endured for forgiveness, opened a way to life that no human heart can conceive, nor mind comprehend. It is all gift, pure and undeserved. It is all grace.

Mercy is the heart of Jesus itself in which we find security and peace. In His merciful heart, we find a home and a refuge. In Him we have life and its fullness. Indeed, He has saved us in mercy and in love.

What an astounding mystery! What a priceless gift! What love!

# Epilogue

## *A Witness on Healing and Forgiveness by Anne Behneman, L.C.S.W.*

F r. Richard M. McAlear has discussed the process of forgiveness, the why, how, and the central role of the Eucharist. I believe it is helpful to consider these concepts as I relate my story of the forgiveness process.

Many people have a problem determining the differences between the concepts of forgiveness and reconciliation. This unclear conceptualization contributes to the confusion that forgiveness is "giving in" or letting down your boundaries one more time, thus allowing the person who previously victimized you to have the power to hurt you again.

Forgiveness is something that we do in our hearts; we release someone from a debt they owe us. We write off the person's debt, and they no longer owe us. We no longer condemn them. Only one party is needed for forgiveness—you. The offending person does not need to ask for it; forgiveness is a work of the heart.

In the forgiveness process, it is important to understand that we do not always achieve reconciliation. God forgave the world, but the whole world is not reconciled to Him. Although He may have forgiven all people, all people have not owned their sin and appropriated His forgiveness. That would be reconciliation. Forgiveness takes one; reconciliation takes two.

We need not allow ourselves to be vulnerable to the offender until we have seen that they have owned their part of the problem. Scripture talks about keeping boundaries with someone until they own what they have done and produce "fruit in keeping with repentance" (Matt. 3:8).

Especially in relationship to God, we must choose to own up to our sin and repent, and then we will be open to receive God's love. It does not necessarily follow that because you have forgiven, you have to reconcile. You can offer reconciliation, but it must be contingent upon the other person owning their behavior and bringing forth trustworthy behavior.

The grieving process is equal to the process of forgiveness when we allow God to walk with us through our grief. When God is not in the grief process, it tends to become self-pity. When God is a part of this process of forgiveness/grieving:

- We stop denying the hurt (denial) and make clear statements about our losses and related feelings, which communicates our pain.
- We stop blaming others, or God, for our hurt (anger) and accept responsibility for our pain.
- We stop making forgiveness conditional (bargaining).
- We let go of self-blame (depression: anger turned on self) and accept God's gift of growth by allowing ourselves to feel the hurt and move through the pain, accepting it as a natural consequence of being in relationship with others (acceptance).

The emotion of anger is part of the forgiveness process. It is very important to remember that forgiveness is not a feeling. Forgiveness begins with a decision, but it is incomplete until our heart has the same felt mercy as Jesus' heart. This is where feeling comes into the process of forgiveness. Like Jesus, we are called to pray for the one who persecutes us.

The heart of forgiveness is that we have been forgiven first, thus we must forgive. We have to love ourselves enough to forgive others, God, and ourselves. It may sound strange, but without forgiveness, we are in emotional and spiritual bondage and not free to love intimately. Until we forgive, we are limited in our ability to share our essence with another. When we accept our forgiveness from God and decide to forgive, we are released from our emotional and spiritual bondage and we know the Lord loves us. This knowledge is the basis of self-love, and all love flows from this knowledge.

## My Personal Story

In my 20's, I was date raped. The fact that I had known this person very well for a long time, along with all the other devastation that goes along with this violation, made the act a tremendous betrayal. I was clearly a Pollyanna and thought things like this did not happen. This moment was the most belief-shattering moment of my life, and in order to survive this trauma, I lost all memory of that night. I did, however, know I was raped because the last scene I remembered was my crying: "No—please don't do this!".

For me, this forgiveness process has been about making many choices at different levels over a time span of 30 years. The deeper the hurt, the more choices you have to make. The good news is that the deeper you go in your forgiveness process, the more you are freed up to love unconditionally.

I was first presented with the choice to forgive at a Healing Mass when my rapist's name came to mind. I knew it was time to forgive—it was my time. God does not ask us to go deep in our forgiveness until it is safe to do so. I began my process of forgiveness and grieving by saying "yes" to God. I wept all through the Mass. The process had begun.

As time passed, there were many sacramental healings, including the healing of shame through the Sacrament of Penance. Grace brought growth and healing.

The next step in the forgiveness process was to stop making forgiveness conditional (bargaining with God). I was involved with the "Idolatry of Why". I was saying: "God, I will forgive if you tell me how he could say he loved me, and then hurt me like this". I was bargaining with God for understanding and God was not playing along. I did not understand—I was not holding any of the cards.

I could not forgive on my own. I would need God's gift of mercy. Only God's mercy could release me from this bondage.

The day came when I was tired of asking "why" and was ready to make another move in the process of forgiveness. I went to my knees and said: "God, I do not have to know why—just give me the grace to forgive". I stopped blaming myself—I stopped bargaining and surrendered to God's will for me. It was then that I moved into acceptance and asked God for the grace to forgive.

The moment I spoke those words, He took me to the foot of the Cross. I was standing at the foot of the

Cross at the moment of forgiveness when Jesus said: "Father, forgive them for they know not what they do". I knew the heart of the truth—I knew I had been forgiven—and I began to cry, knowing that forgiveness was the only choice I could make. Even today, the process is not over. I am a psychotherapist, and as I listen to others' stories, they touch my heart and the process continues.

I have talked mostly about the highs in the process of forgiveness. There have also been many low moments and even days. All have been equally important in this forgiveness/grieving process.

May the Glory of the Father's presence be always with you through both the joys and heartaches of life.